41 thirst-for-knowledge–quenching poems by
CAROL DIGGORY SHIELDS

illustrations by
RICHARD THOMPSON

HANDPRINT BOOKS   **BROOKLYN, NEW YORK**

To Christopher, Ann, Gina, Paula, and Todd
—C.D.S.

For Emma now and Charlotte later
—R.T.

Text copyright © 2002 by Carol Diggory Shields
Illustrations copyright © 2002 by Richard Thompson
Cover and interior design by Karen Kane and Todd Sutherland
All rights reserved
CIP Data is available
All trademark names in this text are the property of their respective owners
BrainJuice is a registered trademark of Handprint Books

Published in the United States in 2002 by Handprint Books
413 Sixth Avenue
Brooklyn, New York 11215
www.handprintbooks.com

First Edition
Printed in the United States of America
ISBN: 1-929766-62-9
2 4 6 8 10 9 7 5 3 1

Dear *Miss Tibbits:*

I was probably the worst student you ever had in all your years of teaching sixth-grade history at North Shore Middle School. I was convinced history was just a lot of boring dates and wars, and tried my best to get the class to agree. Remember the ladybug races? The water balloons?

This is an apology. Not so much for the balloons and the bugs, but for a really rotten attitude. I grew up. I became a poet (believe it or not!). And I learned that history is stories. Stories about people—scared people doing brave things, smart people doing stupid things, people setting off on journeys to unknown destinations, and people risking their lives to help people they'd never even met. There are more interesting, inspiring, funny, and yes, depressing and disgusting stories in American history than I could ever write poems about, but I decided to try. I wanted to write about the times and the people that would have spoken to me, had I been paying attention back in sixth grade. No doubt I have left out a number of really important stories—I know I can count on you to tell me what they are.

And Miss Tibbits, I have done one more thing you may not like: I shortened everything. Why can't you learn about the Boston Tea Party in 17 lines? Or the Louisiana Purchase in 10? Oh dear, I can just hear you sigh. But I have made progress, haven't I?

With fond memories, apologies,
best wishes, and thanks,

Your former student,
Carol Diggory Shields

**First humans cross land-ice bridge
(toll-free) from Siberia to North America**
28,000 B.C.

Ice melts, bridge closes
8,000 B.C.

The First

The first Americans who roamed the prairie
Were kind of big and kind of scary.
Some lived alone, some in a bunch,
A few of them ate the others for lunch.
Some were gentle, some were mean,
Some were spotted or dotted or green.
They hissed and growled and roared great roars—
The first Americans were dinosaurs.

Christopher Columbus arrives
in Bahamas, thinks he has
discovered India
|
1492

Christopher Columbus
arrives in Puerto Rico, thinks
he has discovered Japan
|
1493

Discovery

In fourteen hundred ninety-two,
Columbus did not have a clue;
He sailed to the west, bumped into land:
"Hooray—it's India . . . unless it's Japan,
So I'll call the people Indian folk!"
(The natives thought he was making a joke.)

Next came Vespucci, called Amerigo,
A little bit smarter, he said, "I know,
This is a new place, and with all modesty,
I think we should name it after me."
So with his first name the New World got stuck,
But it could have been worse—

                          he might have been Chuck.

**First permanent English
colony is founded at
Jamestown, called "Jimtown"**

1607

**English colonists prepare
to leave Jimtown**

1609

◄ **8** ►

Colonists decide to stay
following first
tobacco harvest

Before going ashore, Pilgrims
check to see how they look, using
the Mayflower Compact

1611

1620

The Pilgrims

The Pilgrims were grumpy, their clothing was frumpy;
The English king said, "Go away!
To some new location or some other nation,
Where you can pray any old way."

They hired a boat, for weeks they did float
Without a bathroom or even a shower,
No toilet, no tub, no sink for a scrub
(It didn't smell like a mayflower).

The Pilgrims all cheered when land soon appeared,
The captain said, "Wrong place, I fear."
There wasn't a dock, they jumped off on a rock,
"Forget it, we're staying right here!"

Dutchman Peter Minuit buys Manhattan
Island from local Indians.
He thinks they own the land (they don't).

1626

Manhattan

From the Carnarsie Indians, the clever Dutch
Bought some land for not very much.
24 dollars for Manhattan isle!
The Dutchmen signed on the line with a smile,
What a bargain! What a deal!
(You might even say it was a steal.)
But the Dutchmen failed to understand,
That the Carnarsie tribe didn't own the land.

The first American public library
is founded by Benjamin Franklin
(library card, please!)

1731

The first umbrella used in
Windsor, Connecticut, produces
"a riot of merriment and derision"

1740

Recipe

Water (1 harborful),
Sailing ships (3),
1 very dark night,
300 crates tea.
96 colonists
(Mad about taxes,
Dressed up as Indians,
Carrying axes).

British government imposes the Sugar Act, Quartering Act, Currency Act, Townshend Act, Coercive Act, Stamp Act, and Tea Act

1764-73

Boston Tea Party— Revolutionary War is brewing

December 16, 1773

Using the axes,

Smash up the tea,

Dump overboard,

Stir vigorously.

Add some of the crates,

Let brew for a while,

Result?

    1 Tea Party,

    Boston-style.

Explanation

The colonists said, "Tarnation!
We're sick of this aggravation,
Tyranny, taxes, and tariffs—
We want a separation!"

Without further hesitation,
They wrote a brave declaration,
Stating complete independence
From the bossy British nation.

"Egad—what an irritation!"
Sighed the king in exasperation.
(George III didn't understand
The rebels' determination.)

They faced poverty and starvation,
A hopeless situation,
But the ragtag Yankee rebels
Won a hard-fought liberation.

Which is why on our vacation,
We set off a conflagration
With flaming franks and fireworks,
Our Fourth of July celebration!

First comic magazine,
The Wasp, is published

The U.S. purchases the
Louisiana Territory from France—
800,000 sq. miles for $15,000,000.01

1801

1803

The Purchase

Tom Jefferson went shopping for a city, one fine day,
Something in the South, with a harbor or a bay.
"Voila!" said the French, "the city of your dreams!
For only 15 million, we will sell you New Orleans."
"It's very nice," said Tom, "but that's quite a lot to pay."
"Mais non! Not when you hear about our special of the day—
We'll add the Rocky Mountains, the Mississippi shore,
The Great Plains and the bayous, for only one cent more!"
We'll never fill up that much land, thought Tom,
    but what the heck,
"We'll buy it all," he said at last. "Will you take a check?"

**President Jefferson appoints
Lewis and Clark to explore the area
acquired in the Louisiana Purchase**

1803

Job Available

Opening for a teenage girl
(With baby in a pack):
Help lead an expedition
Twelve hundred miles and back,
Translate several languages,
Assist with navigation,
Swim freezing rivers, climb high peaks,
Save group from near-starvation.
Help make peace with hostile tribes,
Work both night and day *

* No vacation, health insurance, benefits, or pay.

1804

THIRD CENSUS: U.S. population reaches 7.2 million, including 1.4 million African-Americans—1.2 million of whom are slaves

1810

Please rise and sing the following poem to the tune of "The Star-Spangled Banner," preferably in three-part harmony.

To the Tune of...

Oh, say can you see, Mr. Francis Scott Key,
Held hostage on board, to keep him out of trouble
As big British ships, sailing in from the sea
Were trying to bomb, Fort McHenry to rubble.
And as he caught sight, in the dawn's early light,
Of the flag waving there, Francis started to write.
A song that was brave, bold, and in-spir-ing—
Sadly set to a tune, that nobody can sing.

WAR OF 1812: U.S. and
Great Britain battle over borders,
trade, and freedom of the seas

1812-1814

Francis Scott Key writes
"The Star-Spangled Banner"

1814

Under the Indian Removal Act, various southeastern tribes
are moved to the west. Thousands die on the journey, and
none was repaid for land, homes, and goods taken.

1816-1858

Trail of Tears

Have you seen the Cherokee?
Lovers of their land, teachers of their children,
They learned the secrets of the written words,
They danced the Eagle Dance.

    We have seen them.
    They passed this way, going west.
    Carrying all they owned, in their arms and on their backs.
    They have not returned.

Construction begins on the Erie Canal, which will connect the Great Lakes and Ohio and Mississippi valleys with the Hudson River and Atlantic Ocean

1817

Have you seen the Choctaw?
Children of Nanih Waiya, the sacred mound,
Singers and poets, planters and harvesters,
They would let no person go hungry.

> We have seen them.
> They passed this way, going west.
> Their old ones were dying, their children cried out.
> They have not returned.

Have you seen the Creek?
Dwellers on the riverbanks, tall and strong,
Ruled by the Beloved Men,
Celebrating the days of the Green Corn.

> We have seen them.
> They passed this way, going west.
> Their food was almost gone, and they had no more.
> They have not returned.

Have you seen the Chickasaw?
Fierce in games and fierce in war,
Proud and tattooed, quick to fight,
Fishers of Mississippi waters.

We have seen them.
They passed this way, going west.
Their feet were bare, and they had no blankets.

They have not returned.

George Washington	John Adams	Thomas Jefferson	James Madison	James Monroe
1789-1797	1797-1801	1801-1809	1809-1817	1817-1825

PRESIDENTS on PARADE
1789   Part I   1845

The presidents are passing by—Stand up and holler!

Number one is Washington,
His picture's on the dollar.
John Adams is next in line,
A smart but grumpy fellow,
Third is Thomas Jefferson,
Builder of Monticello.
Madison is fourth, but first
To call the White House home,
Monroe's doctrine declared:
"Hands off! Leave us alone!"

Adams II was grumpy,
A lot like dear old pop,
Jackson was a country boy
As skinny as a mop.
Van Buren, called "The Fox,"
Was clever, smooth, and slick.
Harrison, at his own parade,
Got sick and died quite quick.
Veep John Tyler took over,
Handsome, tall, and lean,
He must have liked kids a lot,
'Cause he had about fifteen.

**Massachusetts enacts
maximum 10-hour workday
for children under 12**

**First organized
baseball game**

1842

1845

Baseball

It started with a sunny day,
A stick, a ball, a place to play.
A grassy lawn, guys hanging out,
A pitch, crrr-aack, a hit, a shout.
Bases marked with stones or sticks,
"You go first; we'll get last licks."
Then came rules and teams and parks,
Uniforms, lights for the dark,
Leagues and owners, honors, shame,
Heroes, records, scandals, fame.
And still it starts with a sunny day,
A stick and a ball and a place to play.

The Oregon Trail stretches 2,000 miles from Missouri to the Pacific coast. Over 500,000 people make the 5-month journey to the West.

1840s-1860s

Mormons arrive in Utah and found Deseret

1847

Vehicle

Slightly used, all-terrain SUV,
Model year 1843.
Four-oxen drive, convertible roof,
Guaranteed rain- and arrow-proof.

Uncomfortably seats a family of four,
Including furniture, chickens, and more.
Top speed: 50 miles per week
(Faster careening down from a peak).

Music system in stereo,
Fiddle, harmonica, one old banjo.
Four sturdy tires of wood and steel
For that bouncy off-road feel.

Driven to Oregon (just one way),
Make an offer and take it away!

The Underground Railroad is a secret
network of routes to help slaves escape
to Canada, where they could live in freedom

1830-1865

Massachusetts
declares
Christmas legal

1856

This Train

The passengers are hidden,
The conductors are on guard.
The stations secret places—
A cellar, a barn, a yard.
The train tracks are invisible,
Hope is the engineer,
The final stop is freedom
From slavery and fear.

**Supreme Court rules
that African-Americans
are not U.S. citizens**

|

1857

**Pony Express begins overland
mail service from Missouri
to California**

|

1860

Confederates open fire on Fort
Sumter in Charleston, South
Carolina, beginning the Civil War

Emancipation Proclamation
is issued, freeing all slaves

April 12, 1861

1863

Civil War

Harper's Ferry,
Shiloh,
Picket's Mill,
Seven Pines,
Appomattox,
Malvern Hill.
Vicksburg,
Atlanta,
Battle of Bull Run.
Names like the beat
Of a muffled drum.

**President Lincoln is assassinated;
Lee surrenders the Confederate Army to Grant;
the Thirteenth Amendment abolishes slavery**

1865

Cedar Mountain,
Mossy Creek,
Bloody Bridge,
Nashville,
Saltville,
Indian Ridge.
Chickamauga,
Tupelo,
Gettysburg.
Their names are the words
Of a funeral dirge.

Face to face,
Side by side,
We fought ourselves.
Many of us died.

Mr. Seward's Folly

Alaska? I ask ya, who wants such a place?

So cold it freezes the nose off your face.

Tons of ice and miles of snow,

A place where no one wants to go.

What's that you say? It might have gold?

Quick, Mr. Seward, mark it "SOLD!"

The U.S. becomes
the world's foremost
industrial nation

1870-1900

Record number of immigrants
(some 9 million) arrive
in the U.S.

1880-1900

Revolution

It started with Eli's cotton gin
That made cotton easy to pick and spin,
Then the jenny spun thread, clickity-clack,
And the weaving loom shuttled forward and back,
The mill wheels whirled, thumped, and whined,
Turning out goods of every kind.
It grew and grew, an enormous need—
"Give us more power! Give us more speed!"
Huffing and chuffing, engines of steam,
Billows of smoke and whistles that scream,
Riverboats, steamboats, great iron trains,
Churning upriver, chugging through plains.
Faster and faster—no turning back,
Change came barreling down the track.

**Dedication of the
Statue of Liberty**

1886

**During the Spanish-American War Colonel
Theodore Roosevelt comes to national
attention in charge on San Juan Hill**

1898

PRESIDENTS ON PARADE
1845 Part II 1889

Here comes Polk, number eleven,
Added land all kinds of ways,
Followed by Zachary Taylor,
Our chief for five hundred days.
Number thirteen was Fillmore,
Sent the Navy to Japan,
Next was "Handsome Frank,"
Mr. Pierce, a good-looking man.
Along came James Buchanan,
Looked around and said, "Uh-oh!
The Civil War is brewing,
I think I'd better go!"
So Lincoln, Honest Abe,
Faced a troubled nation,

Freed slaves throughout the land,
With his Proclamation.
Seventeen, Andrew Johnson,
Got himself impeached,
Ulysses Grant was very shy,
And never gave a speech.
Hayes married "Lemonade Lucy,"
Garfield was shot and died,
Next came "Elegant Arthur,"
His whiskers were his greatest pride.
Then came Grover Cleveland,
Who returned for an encore,
He was president twenty-two,
And also twenty-four.

Teddy

The President said, "Beware!
I'm out to bag a bear."
His guide said, "Over there!
I see one in his lair."
Said Roosevelt, "I declare,
That's just a baby bear—
Hunting it would be unfair!"
The news spread from here to there
That Teddy had spared a bear,
Which is in your bed upstairs,
In cribs, on sofas, in chairs,
Or almost anywhere
You will find a teddy bear.

Poor You

Oh poor, poor you!

All that homework you must do,
And then there are the chores—
Feed the dog, sweep the floors.
Don't you wish that you
Lived in nineteen-oh-two?

Only three short months in school!
(Now that sounds really cool),
And throughout the other nine,
You'd be working in a mine,
Thirteen hours every day
(No summers off
    or time for play).

2 DAYS
WITHOUT AN
ACCIDENT!
KEEP UP THE
GOOD WORK!

Or maybe you'd rather chill
By working in a mill,
Tending a huge machine
That spits dirt and grease and steam.
Dawn to dark, rain or shine,
Each day you'd earn one thin dime!

Don't you wish that you
Lived in nineteen-oh-two?

Kitty Hawk

There once were two brothers—crazy guys,
Who wished that people could fly,
    Folks said, "By cracky,
      Those Wright boys are wacky,"
Till they looked up and saw them fly by.

San Francisco, 1906

Under the earth, a sleeping giant lies,
Over him, people, as busy as ants,
Built houses, roads, bridges, and towers.
Until one day the giant turned,
And twitched in his sleep,
Shrugged off the houses, bridges, roads, and towers,
And turning again, went back to sleep.
While, busy as ants, the people started building
Houses, roads, bridges, and towers.

**Surfing is introduced
in California**

**Henry Ford develops
the assembly line method
of producing automobiles**

**Kool-Aid drink mix
first made available**

1910

1913

1914

The Great War

The First World War,

War of stinking trenches, endless mud,

Ceaseless boom of cannon, the rockets' scream,

Clanking tanks and droning planes,

The rattle of machine-gun fire.

And then in the eleventh month,

On the eleventh day,

At the eleventh hour,

Silence.

Peace.

The U.S. enters "The Great War"	Influenza hits the U.S. and the rest of the world; 550,000 people die	The Armistice ends "The Great War"
1917	1918	1918

The Eighteenth Amendment
to the Constitution prohibits
liquor in the U.S.

1919

The Nineteenth Amendment
to the Constitution gives
women the right to vote

1920

Women Get the Vote!

The Declaration writers goofed—
All men created equal?
A hundred and forty years went by
Till they fixed it with a sequel.

There would have been a lot less fuss,
No strife, no fights, no dramas,
If the founding fathers had listened
To the founding mamas.

A Pennsylvania law requires
skirts to be at least four
inches below the knee
|
1921

Lindbergh flies nonstop
across Atlantic in
Spirit of St. Louis
|
1927

The Roaring Twenties

In the twenties, guys were dapper,
A girl who was wild was called a flapper.
Girls so wild, that, oh my dears,
They cut their hair up to their ears!
Still more shocking, oh my stars,
Some of them drove motorcars,
Wore skirts so short that, golly gees,
You could almost see their knees!
Put on powder, lipstick too,
Said things like, "Twenty-three, skiddoo!"
It's a good thing, I must say,
That girls don't act like that today.

Seven members of Al Capone's
rival bootlegger gang are
murdered in Chicago

February 14, 1929

Prohibition

Prohibition—not a great idea,
It didn't stop people from drinking beer,
They just brewed up their own at home,
Or bought it from bad guys like Al Capone.

Depressing Depression

Money gone, jobs were scarce,
Banks were repossessing,
The Great Depression, all in all,
Was pretty darn depressing.

Franklin Delano Roosevelt is
inaugurated as president

1933

The most flouted law in history,
Prohibition, is repealed

1933

FDR's ABC

FDR, down in DC,
Said, "We'll end this depression, ASAP.
The CCC and the WPA
Will give folks jobs right away,
While the SSA and the SEC
Will fix the broken economy.
There's the AAA for the farmer's hay,
Electric power from the REA,
With the TVA and PWA,
Soon the USA will be A-OK."

PRESIDENTS ON PARADE
1889   Part III   1945

Hooray for Harrison, twenty-three,
(His granddad was number nine),
Poor McKinley, twenty-five,
Was killed shaking hands in a line.
Next came Teddy Roosevelt,
(Famous for the bears),
With a bunch of kids who slid
Down the White House stairs.
Taft, twenty-seven,
A big man—super-size.

Wilson was a scholar,
And won the Nobel Prize.
Harding and pals played poker,
Carousing through the night,
Next, tall "Silent Cal" Coolidge,
Kept his lips buttoned tight.
Herbert Hoover, thirty-one,
The Depression brought him grief,
Next FDR came along,
His New Deal spelled relief.

The Japanese bomb Pearl Harbor. U.S. declares war on Germany and Japan in the days that follow.

Victory in Europe, "V-E Day"

December 7, 1941

May 8, 1945

World War II

In our very own galaxy, not long ago,
An evil empire began to grow.
Hitler, Tojo, Mussolini,
Each worse than a movie meanie,
Three dictators with a single goal:
"We want the world under our control!"
But they were defeated, not by computers,
Spaceships, or intergalactic shooters,
Or robot weapons or laser spears,
But by men and women,
 and their blood, sweat, and tears.

The world's first
electronic digital computer
is developed
|
1946

All-New ENIAC!

Be the first one on your block,
Get a computer for your home!
30 tons of lights and buttons,
Wires, tubes, and chrome.
It'll balance your family budget,
Help you do your math,
Solve complicated problems
In an hour and a half!
Buy the ENIAC computer!
Though it's bigger than your house,
Just move into the backyard,
With your children, pets, and spouse.

Jukeboxes go into
mass production

Roswell incident
(supposed alien landing in New Mexico)

1946

1947

Fun in the Forties

Hooray for Saturday night—
We get to stay up late,
Race through dinner, clean up quick,
"Hurry kids, the program won't wait!"
Mom on the sofa, Dad in his chair,
Only one minute to go—
Until, at last, Dad leans over
And turns on the radio!

Bomb shelter plans become
widely available in
government pamphlets | The Korean War | Diet soda
is introduced

1950s | 1950-1953 | 1952

Fun in the Fifties

The year is 1952,
Television is very new,
A picture the size of a goldfish bowl,
That ripples, zigzags, flips, and rolls.
No satellite dishes—just rabbit ears,
Sometimes a show just disappears.
Wow! Three channels to choose at night,
Broadcast in glorious black-and-white.
Snow and static and "ghosts" on the screen—
The coolest thing we'd ever seen.

Please sit on the floor to sing the following poem to the tune of "The Wheels on the Bus," preferably using appropriate hand gestures.

The Wheels on the (Montgomery) Bus

The driver on the bus said, "Move on back!
Move on back, move on back!
White folk in front and black in back,
All through the town."

Rosa L. Parks said, "I won't move,
I won't move, I won't move.
I'll stay right here
    where I sat down,
All through the town."

**The Supreme Court declares that
Alabama's state and local laws requiring
segregation on buses are illegal**

1956

The policemen said, "You're under arrest,
Under arrest, under arrest."
The policemen said, "You're under arrest,
We're taking you downtown."

The people all said, "Don't ride the bus,
Make a peaceful fuss, but don't ride the bus.
We'll carpool, bike, or walk if we must,
All through the town."

One year later . . .

The people on the bus sit wherever they like,
Wherever they like, wherever they like.
Black and tan and brown and white,
All through the town.

Cold War

There once was a war nobody lost,
A war that nobody won.
Don't know just when it started,
Or just when it was done.
But in a war with Russia,
Against the USA,
I'd rather have a cold war
Than a hot one, any day.

The Soviet Union launches *Sputnik* I
and *Sputnik* II, the beginning
of the "space race"

1957

U.S. postal rates go up;
a first-class stamp
costs four cents

1958

Space Race

It's the U.S. and Russia in a race for space,
Russia sends up Sputnik, grabs first place.
Then two more Sputniks—
　　Russia is sizzling!
The U.S. rockets are all just fizzling.
At last we launch a satellite,
But Russia's ahead with a
　　manned space flight!

The Mercury Seven step up to bat,
It's neck and neck, and tit for tat.
Russia goes to the moon and circles around,
Then the U.S. scores big—Apollo touchdown!

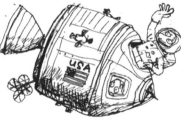

We still could be racing to this very day,
But we finally discovered a much better way,
Exploring together the last frontier,
Side by side on the space station MIR.

Dangerous

The grown-ups said, "Oh no, no, no!
This stuff is very bad!
It will warp your mind and make you deaf
And surely drive you mad."
They panned it and they banned it,
Kids listened anyway.
In spite of all the warnings,
Rock 'n' roll was here to stay.

First demonstration
against U.S. involvement
in Vietnam

1965

First rock music festival
in Monterey, California

1967

Groovy

I'm looking so groovy
In this patched denim skirt,
Platform sandals,
Tie-dyed T-shirt,
Bangles and beads,
And rings for my toes.
I'm glad my mom kept
All her great '60s clothes.

Martin Luther King, Jr. (April)
and Robert F. Kennedy (June)
are assassinated

1968

Democratic National Headquarters
are burglarized
for political information

1972

Vietnam

The questions linger on and on,
Who was right and who was wrong?
Why did we go, why did we fight?
Who was wrong and who was right?
Vietnam—to leave or stay?
To fight, to flee, or to obey?
The answers cloaked in shades of gray,
The questions never go away.

After a long congressional inquiry
into the Watergate burglaries,
Nixon resigns presidency

Last U.S. troops leave
Vietnam

1974

1975

Watergate

Tricky Dick Nixon hired some spies,
Thought he would bug the other guys,
But he got caught, with no escape,
Trapped by his own recording tape.

The Space Shuttle Challenger
explodes 73 seconds after launch

January 28, 1986

The world braces itself for computer
failure at the turn of the century

December 31, 1999

Y2K

We're all prepared for Y2K,

Got firewood, water, and food stashed away.

At the stroke of midnight, there is no doubt,

The electrical power will surely go out.

Computers will crash, systems will fail,

No more phones, TV, or mail.

We'll grow our own food, live off the land,

Cook over a fire, sew clothes by hand.

You say it's past midnight
and everything's fine?

Well, um, er, ah,

then—never mind.

George W. Bush wins the 2000 election by 4 electoral votes; loses the popular vote. R.B. Hayes wins 1876 electoral election by 1 vote; loses the popular vote.

2000

CLOSE CALLS

Close Call I

The election was too close to call,
The count went on for days,
And, finally, a winner, by just one vote,
President Rutherford B. Hayes.

Close Call II

The election was too close to call,
Votes were counted, and counted anew,
The court stepped in, a winner declared.
The Prez? George Bush, number two.

Harry S Truman	Dwight D. Eisenhower	John F. Kennedy	Lyndon B. Johnson	Richard M. Nixon
1945-1953	1953-1961	1961-1963	1963-1969	1969-1974

PRESIDENTS ON PARADE 1945 Part IV

Truman stopped the buck,
Ike had general's stars,
Kennedy left too soon,
Johnson showed his scars.
Thirty-seven was Nixon,
Watergate did him in,
Ford was next, then Carter
With his famous grin.
Number forty, Reagan,
Star of movies and TV,
George Bush, the dad, was next,
"Please! No broccoli!"

Clinton at age 46,
Was number forty-two,
Followed by George W.,
And his cowboy crew.

Presidents marching
Down through the years,
To waves and hoorays
And boos and cheers.

Over 3,000 are killed in terrorist attacks
on the World Trade Center in New York
City and the Pentagon in Washington, D.C.

September 11, 2001

The Lady

I know a lady, you might know her too,
She's seen a lot in her years.
Joyful reunions and sad good-byes,
Laughter, sighs, and tears.
She saw the towers' awful fall,
The smoke burned in her eyes.
She saw the fear and saw the grief,
The hope, the prayers, the cries.

And soon she saw the work begin,
A country unified,
She saw neighbor helping neighbor,
She saw a proud flag rise.
She saw it all from where she stands,
Beautiful and tall,
And still she holds her torch up high,
And still she welcomes all.

Title Index